Lessons
Life Taught Me

A Teenage Girl's Guide to Adulthood

Stacy L. Moore

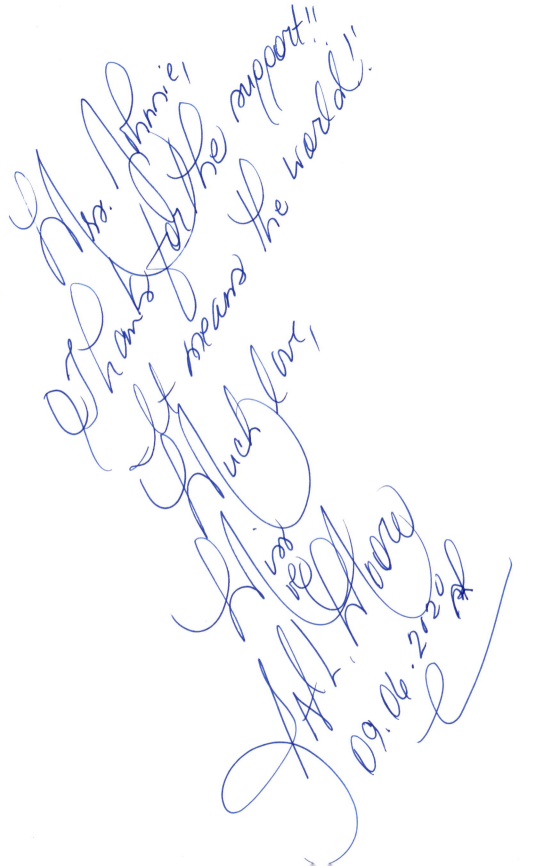

Mrs. Annie!

Thanks for the support!!
It means the world!

Much love,

09.06.2020

DEDICATION

This book is dedicated to the memory of my oldest sister, Kelly Savage, who would have bought the first 100 copies just to prove her support; to my son, Jhmarquias Newsome, who has given me endless encouragement from the point of conception of this idea until its birth; to my three "grannies," Kody, A'Zylia, and Peyton, who give me purpose and hope; to my parents, Josie & Garlee Claiborne, my sister Tammie Stewart, my brother Garlee, Jr., and the rest of my family for their unwavering faith in me; to all of the students who have crossed my path in the last 20 years for allowing me to play a role in their journey to adulthood; and finally to my cousin, T'Ambria "5" Shinall, for pushing me to continue this ambitious undertaking even when I questioned myself.

Thanks, and much love,

Table of Contents

Introduction

"Let the words of my mouth, and the meditation of my heart, be acceptable in thy sight, O Lord, my strength, and my redeemer."

Psalm 19:14

Although watching their children grow up is scary for many parents, most children "can't wait to get grown." They eagerly anticipate their independence so they can experience life on their own terms. Very seldom, however, do these children consider the inherent hiccups that occur with growing up, and often they don't fully understand just what it means to "get grown." They assume adulthood, i.e. being grown, simply means turning 18 and saying, "I'm grown." They think doing grown-up things is the same as being grown! Real grown people, however, know that adulthood isn't as easy as it seems because being grown removes the safety net that our parents placed beneath us and places the full weight of financial and social responsibility on our shoulders. I wish I had a dime for every student who came back and said they wish they could "go back and be a child again" because being grown "is too hard." I'd be rich by now. Being grown means you have a home and an address separate from your parents. Being grown means your bills are in your own name, and you are responsible for paying those bills -- or suffering the consequences when you don't. Being grown is not a state of mind; it is a state of action.

Maturing from adolescence to adulthood affects more than our physical states. Throughout the process, our emotional, social, and psychological states are also altered. Although adolescence itself is a natural stage of life, dealing with the constant changes that accompany it does not always occur as naturally.

Over 30 years ago, my life as a high school student was filled with its share of ups and downs, but nothing I faced was as daunting or as challenging as teens face today. The biggest challenge my friends and I faced was trying to make our hand-me-downs look as new as the clothes our middle-class peers wore. Today, however, teens face many more emotionally debilitating issues. They are bombarded with images of false perfection in the media, and they are faced with the mounting pressure of trying to look perfect because of it. Because many of them don't possess adequate coping skills, they often internalize their problems until they become emotionally paralyzed, which makes focusing on anything else virtually impossible.

Working closely with teens as a high school teacher for the past 20 years has afforded me countless opportunities to witness the endless emotional uncertainties that many teens, specifically females, undergo. It is easy to say these teens are "just too grown" or "too hyperactive" so we can medicate them whenever possible. Medicating them, however, is like prescribing candy for a bacterial infection. Both decisions are ineffective because neither addresses the core problem, and effective therapy requires locating the nucleus of the issue before treatment options are ever evaluated.

I held several positions before I began my career in education, and although teaching has not been without its own share of stressors, it has, by far, been my most fulfilling job. I get to teach and be taught by a myriad of young children, who simply yearn for someone to be a compass for them on their road to adulthood. Many of them struggle, as I did when I was a teenager, to find a place where they fit, so I challenge them to not fit, but to fix a place where they are comfortable being themselves. My profession requires I teach them the conventions of Standard English, but my humanity mandates I try to help them navigate the murky waters to adulthood so they can become productive citizens who are confident in their own skins.

The idea of this book was born out of desperation for the many young girls who fill my classroom every day with some issue or another that has drained their mental, emotional, and/or social energy. My heart aches for them because they are trying to cross the murky waters of pre-adulthood barefoot. These girls don't trust easily, so most of them keep their uncertainties and questions bottled up because they fear public ridicule or persecution. It is not until the bottle becomes too full and the children "act-out" that adults pay closer attention.

I neither profess nor insinuate any expertise in the field of human psychology as I have very limited formal education in the discipline, but I do possess the inevitable wisdom that is bred from 20 years of being educated by teens – the kind of wisdom that cannot be found in a textbook or taught in a classroom. Thus, it is my heartfelt prayer that this book will help young ladies empty their bottles so their transition to adulthood becomes a little less scary. If I had had a book like this or someone with whom I felt comfortable enough to share my questions and insecurities when my bottle starts to overflow as a teen, I probably would have avoided some of the many pitfalls and potholes that cluttered my path to adulthood.

This book is filled with lessons I wish I'd been taught when I was a teen. As it was, I learned many of them after I became an adult, and most of them I had to teach myself. So, it is my hope that this book opens the currents of communication for young girls as they realize other teens are dealing with similar growing pains and they don't have to figure things out alone.

Thanks in advance for your consideration and patronage.

Stacy

Just As I Am: A Poem by Stacy L. Moore.

See me for who I am
and not for whom you think I should be.
Accept me ***Just as I Am***
because The Great God Almighty handmade me.

Some may wish for the wisdom of Solomon,
and some may long for the patience of Job,
but I am satisfied with me ***Just as I Am***
because I am one of God's handmade souls.

I don't have the riches of Pharaoh
nor the glory of St. Paul,
but my God blesses me anyway
in spite of my sins, my faults, my shortcomings and all

If I could be anybody else,
I would still be just me
because God created me in His own image,
and my inner beauty and worth He can surely see

So, ***Just as I Am***
I am satisfied still
for I know God created NO mistakes

and I am assured His love for me is real.

1999

Lesson 1: *Know that you're worthy.*

This is the first lesson because it is not only the most important, but it is also the hinge and glue for all of the other lessons. I didn't grasp the full significance of this lesson until I became an adult, so I floundered around a lot as a teen and young adult. If young ladies can grasp the magnitude of this lesson early, they can avoid a lot of undue stress in the future.

"If you ain't worthy just raise your hands/And let me know that you understand/That we are all so blessed to be loved, loved…

Stand for Him or fall for anything/'Cause through

His eyes we all look the same/…

Feels like I always fall short of being worthy/'Cause I ain't good enough/But He still loves me"

Beyonce' "He Still Loves Me"

In a world often dominated by the media's idea of perfection, it is so easy to become uncomfortable in your own skin. Society's idea of what's beautiful and what's not can be rather strict and is oftentimes so inflexible that many females question not only their appearance but their worth as well. Adolescence is a time of uncertain growth all by itself; but when you factor in all the other stuff teenagers undergo, like peer pressure, body image issues, sexual awareness/awakening, and this period of a young girl's journey to adulthood can be downright frightening.

Every year, I meet young girls who become consumed with fitting into the mold of perfection that society has created. It's obvious in the 26-inch, 200-dollar hair extensions. It's evident in the colored contact lenses. It's visible in the mile-long acrylic nails and eyelashes. Before you get offended, I am not suggesting that there is anything wrong with wearing these things; and because it is not my money, you're probably wondering why I even care. Honestly, I don't. My concern is more for the façade and the fakeness that these things perpetuate. Let's be honest. A lot of the girls who wear weave already have long hair. They just want the weave because "everybody is wearing it." They also have pretty eyes, and simple mascara would provide enough umph to garner attention. Still, many of them wear these things likely because society and celebrities suggest they are necessary if a woman wants to feel beautiful, i.e. if she wants to feel worthy. To the skilled eye, however, these cosmetic "necessities" seem to suggest that the girls are not comfortable being their bare selves. This is not true for every young girl, but it is for a lot of them. Still, I am more concerned about those girls who cannot afford such expenses because they are the ones who are ridiculed and slammed for not wearing/having such things. So, I have to wonder if we are suggesting that these girls are less worthy because they don't wear them. Are we suggesting girls are not worthy unless they are "enhanced" by outside stuff? Are we perpetuating the concept of beauty by any means necessary? Are we saying girls should want to look a certain way regardless of the cost, and I don't mean "cost" in terms of money?

Case in point: One of my young girls complained about her eyelids suddenly swelling. Because she was wearing eyelash extensions, I asked if she thought the swelling had anything to do with the glue that she used for her lashes. She said it could be, so I suggested she just not wear the lashes for a few days. She acted as if I had cursed her. She said, "Miss Moe, Ain't no way I'm coming to school without my lashes." I thought she was joking, so I said, "You will if you can't see for a few days." She said, "[Main], you just don't understand. There's just something about wearing lashes and weave...when you put them on, you just feel so pretty." I gawked at her in stunned silence. She laughed at my expression, but I asked what she would do if a doctor told her to stop wearing them because they could negatively impact her vision. Her thoughtful response? "Oh well...somebody will help me...somebody will tell me what's on the board." I imagine I really looked like a deer caught in headlights then. I asked, "So you don't mind being blind as long as you're pretty?" She simply shrugged her shoulders and went back to her assignment. Even now, years later, I'm still speechless. Don't get me wrong. I do understand the pressure that society puts on women to look a certain way, but my student's I-don't-care reaction to the possibility of negatively impacting her eyesight shocked me. When, how, had we become a society where the idea of perfection trumps common sense? Have we become a society where appearances mean more than reality? Do we want to be a society that teaches future generations that their worth is connected to how they look? I surely hope not, but I'm not sure if or how we can avoid it?

(Allow me to regress for a moment.)

I am the third child of four born into a family that

many deemed lower-class and/or poor. I, however, reject both adjectives because although we didn't have a lot of money and material possessions, we still had a lot more than some people. Despite, or perhaps because of our economic state, my parents always stressed that material possessions cannot add to or subtract from a person's worth. That argument sounded great – until I was in the presence of opinionated, mean-spirited children who could afford nicer, more expensive things. It seemed as if somebody was always making fun of me because of what I didn't have. I pretended it didn't bother me, but I remember looking at those kids with envy as I wondered how it would feel to have such nice things. I think that is where my academic drive came from. That is why I worked so hard to make A's and B's in school. I wanted a future where I could wear nice, expensive things. As the third daughter, I usually ended up with the clothes my older sisters outgrew; but even when I was fortunate enough to get new clothes (usually for Christmas since my grades were good), I seldom felt worthy because my classmates still found something to joke about. So, even in brand new clothes, I questioned my worth.

To make matters worse, in addition to not being able to afford the latest fashions and shoes, I wasn't blessed with features that many consider beautiful. My lips are thick, my nose is wide, and my hair is kinky – pretty standard physical characteristics for a lot of African Americans. Still, during my adolescent years, it was these physical traits that made me shun the limelight and shrink under others' perusal of me. Although I excelled in academics, I went through school avoiding extra attention because I thought I was unworthy since I wore basic clothes and I wasn't drop-dead gorgeous.

The first time I thought I might be worthy was during middle school when one of my teachers took notice of my situation and tried to help. I am eternally indebted to Mrs. Brenda Joyce Shepphard, my middle school science teacher and local renowned beautician, because she had no idea that when she simply offered to fix my hair, she had given me the lifeline I so desperately needed. I had been the proverbial thorn in her side – nasty attitude, noncompliant disposition, and a sharp, sarcastic tongue; but she didn't allow any of my false bravado to perturb her. Instead, she looked beneath my icky-ness and saw the conflicted, insecure little girl I was. So throughout middle and high school, Mrs. Shepphard selflessly made sure my hair was always presentable, and she even bought me clothes. She never bragged about what she did; and even when my mom was able to offer her a token of our appreciation, she seldom accepted it. She likely had no idea just how life-changing her kindness was and how it still inspires me. I don't know why she chose me, but I'm forever grateful that she did. Perhaps she recognized my worth long before I did.

It wasn't until my senior year in high school that my confidence really started to shift in a positive way, but even then it was slow. One day, we were summoned to see who was interested in competing for homecoming queen. I had not even considered the possibility, but when the sponsor called my name, without thought, I said, "Yes." Several of the more popular girls seemed more surprised by my response than I was, but I had put my foot in my mouth, and my pride wouldn't let me remove it. We couldn't afford fancy dresses or gowns, so my mother called several coworkers until she finally found me a dress. Mrs. Shepphard did my hair, and my sister did my makeup –nothing nearly as fancy as what kids wear today, but it was definitely a huge step up from my usual appearance. I remember being so nervous, but the support from my family and friends made me feel special. I felt worthy. I didn't win the crown, but I did place third. You would have thought I had won the state title though. My family and friends were so proud, and people who had never seemed to notice my existence finally saw me. I wasn't suddenly Miss Popularity, but I was stoked enough to believe I was worthy of such an accomplishment.

After I graduated from high school, I enrolled in Tougaloo College, where both my confidence and self-awareness blossomed. I was still the same average-looking girl on the outside, but a newfound appreciation for my uniqueness was slowing dawning on the inside. My dad was strict, so I hadn't been allowed to do a lot of stuff while I was in high school. Tougaloo became my gateway to independence and freedom. I, like most teenagers, was excited to be grown because I could finally experience life without having to worry about what my dad would say or do. I partied and dallied in things I dare not mention here because I still fear my dad's wrath and he may read this. Let's just say I was enjoying life to the fullest! I was able to go and come as I pleased. I could go to clubs and hang out for as long as I wanted – without worry!! That kind of unchecked freedom doesn't come without consequences though. I went from a 3.7 GPA to virtually failing all of my classes. I had completely lost my focus, and my ambition had been replaced by apathy. I didn't care about anything except enjoying my newfound freedom. If I had not become pregnant during my last year at Tougaloo, I cringe to think what my life would have become. I didn't plan my pregnancy, and my son's father and I were never in a committed relationship. We were simply doing grown-up things, which led to grown-up consequences. Still, when I saw my son's profile during my first sonogram, I knew my life would never be the same. I re-discovered my drive, re-focused my agenda, and returned to Tougaloo College determined to provide a better life for my child.

After Marqus was born, I tried to make sure that every time we left home, he was "camera-ready." I literally planned his wardrobe to ensure people ooh and aah-ed when they saw him. At the time, I thought I was being a good mother; but now – 25 years later – I must admit that I was simply working to keep my insecurities concealed. I figured if people were focused on Marqus, they wouldn't have time to focus on me. I wanted Marqus to have everything I didn't have when I was a child. I wanted him to never know the shame of being mocked or criticized for not having the latest fashions and shoes, so I gave him everything I possibly could. What I've learned as both a parent and a teacher, however, is that that kind of overcompensation often does more harm than good. It breeds a sense of entitlement in the child, and it almost always stunts ambition. As a student, I overachieved because I wanted the same luxuries my classmates seemed to have. Marqus, on the other hand, had virtually everything he could want, so he – like so many young children – lacked the desire and drive to achieve more than the minimum even though he was capable of more. He saw no need to strive for excellence when he was already being rewarded for mediocrity, which was mostly my fault, not his.

If you don't have a lot of material possessions or can't afford them right now, don't stress about it. Instead, allow not having those things to inspire you. Allow it to motivate you to dig deeper and try harder when you want to give up. Allow it to encourage you to study harder and earn better grades so you can have the future you want. Just know that having such things may not be as fulfilling as you expect it to be.

Loving Marqus was easy; it took absolutely no effort. Loving myself, on the other hand, was not so effortless. It took years of practice and even more patience. I had to constantly affirm and validate my own worth, which wasn't easy because I could not escape the insecurities and inadequacies I secretly harbored. I may have been skinning and grinning on the outside, but I was trying hard to hold it together on the inside. I wrote "Just As I Am: A Poem" years ago in response to my mom's innocent critique of my appearance. I have what older people call "bow-hips," and it is virtually impossible to hide them. I hadn't been teaching long, and though I was dressed professionally, my mother said my thighs looked "wide" and I needed to dress "better around them students." Although I knew she meant no harm, I internalized her comments, and for the next few months or so, I wrestled with how to dress so that I looked worthy of being a teacher. It was around that time, though, that I had started actively reading The Bible, and I was familiar with a few Scriptures. The one that resonated deeply within my heart at that time was Genesis 1: 26-28 (KJV), which proclaims, "...And God said, Let us make man in our image, after our likeness...So God created man in His own image, in the image of God created He him; male and female created He them…and God blessed them…" Those words spoke new life into my near-empty soul and allowed me to see not my faults and failures when I looked in the mirror, but God's own image. Those words helped me recognize my worth as a handmade creation of The Ultimate Creator. After a lot of internal debating and even more attempts to neutralize my physical appearance, I realized there was not much I could do to fix myself so that everybody would be pleased, so I had to accept myself – just as I am – before I could expect others to do so. That's not to suggest that my confidence suddenly peaked or that it didn't waver because it did–and it still does. Even today, when I look in the mirror and see my physical imperfections, I still have to recite affirmations to convince myself that I am indeed worthy – regardless of how I look.

So, regardless of your physical imperfections; regardless of material possessions (or the lack thereof); regardless of the amount of money you have (or don't have); regardless of the type of home in which you live; regardless of the type of neighborhood where you live; regardless of anything that is not within you, know that you are worthy!! You are worthy because you were created by the Ultimate Creator, and everything He created is worthy. So go on and celebrate your worth. It is okay to be your own biggest fan and your own loudest cheerleader because if you don't believe you're worth it, who will?

Lesson 2: *Eliminate excuses*

"You can have results or excuses, but not both."

Arnold Schwarzenegger

"I would have done it, but…" "I couldn't do it because…" "You just don't know how hard things are for me." "Well my mother/father ain't in my life…" "I wanted to do it but…" "If I had it easy like…has it, I would/could…"

Life is unforgiving, time is fleeting, and responsibility is inevitable. These are hard facts, but excuses still abound. When we don't want to do something, when things don't go our way, when we haven't done what we should or could have, we find excuses; and excuses are seldom hard to find. In adulthood, however, we have to eliminate excuses and accept ownership and responsibility for our own actions if we want to see results.

Neither of my parents graduated from high school because they had to drop out of school to help support their families. Still, my siblings and I could not use our parents' lack of formal education as an excuse because getting a high school diploma was a non-negotiable in my dad's house. After high school, we either had to go to college, join the military, or get a job. There was no acceptable excuse for not being productive at something. Today, however, ambition does not seem to be as valued or as valuable among teens and young adults. Any excuse to be average or less is acceptable. Many of my students, despite their youth and inexperience, carry a lot of unnecessary baggage because they have not been equipped with the necessary tools to deal with their *stuff*, so they create excuses for their inadequacies. I often tell parents that we adults are partially at fault for our children's inability to maneuver life as capable, independent young adults. We want our children to have it easier than we had it and to be better than we are. We try to protect them from as many hardships as we can, so we don't give them the opportunity to figure out how to rescue themselves when they get in a tight spot. We try to keep them from falling, but when they do, we immediately pick them up, dust them off, and kiss their tears away. Giving them so many things and not allowing them to learn how to save themselves, however, simply make creating and using excuses that much easier. Our real, true duty as parents is to train and prepare our children as well as we can, facilitate their growth (*without* hand-delivering them excuses or saving them from every downfall), and be a safe haven where they can recuperate when life gets hard. Okay, I've digressed again – back to eliminating excuses.

Many of my students have excuses ready for just

about anything they face. They have an excuse for why they don't have something, for why they don't know something, or why they can't do something. When it comes to something they *want* to have/know/do, however, the outcome is just the opposite. When it's something they want, they neither make nor accept excuses. Instead, they work tirelessly until they get what they want. Case in point: Many of my students have cell phones, and they quickly teach themselves how to use these cell phones to navigate social media and even to cheat in class; but many of them don't use those gadgets for more practical purposes. A 17-year-old student once asked me to teach him how to tell time. I was shocked and humbled. I was shocked because at 17 he didn't know how to tell time *and* because he wasn't embarrassed by his lack of knowledge of such a simple thing. Still, I was humbled because he asked *me* to teach him. When I asked why he didn't know how to tell time, quite naturally he offered an excuse: "They didn't teach us," and "Nobody showed me how to do it." Humility aside, I forced him, at 17, to accept responsibility *and* blame for his own lack of knowledge. I asked him if he had a cell phone? "Yes, ma'am." Did he know how to use it? "Yes, ma'am." Did he ever use YouTube or Google? "Yes, ma'am." While I knew he probably had not been formally taught how to tell time in school, I would not be denied. So, I asked who taught him how to use his cell phone. I asked who taught him how to navigate YouTube and Google? Who trained him to use social media? Just as I assumed, he admitted he had taught himself. He was happy to boast that he had just gotten his phone and "figured it out." When I then asked why he had not used his phone to learn how to tell time, he was speechless. I took my phone, went to YouTube, and began typing "how to tell time." Before I could even finish the phrase, several entries appeared. The student was speechless -- *again*. I told him he has to eliminate excuses if he really wants to be successful. I also reminded him that he was mere months from turning 18, that age when society expects him to have mastered a few things, so he had to rely more on himself and less on others for what he wants/needs to know. He thanked me for the lesson and assured me he'd "do better."

Lately, I've been approached by quite a few students who are the product of one-parent households, and many of these students try to use who is or is not involved in their lives as an excuse for their shortcomings. Although I lived with both of my parents as a teenager, I can still empathize with these students because I raised Marqus as a single-parent. It's so amazing how something that seems so normal can have such a major impact on a person's sense of worth. I remember talking with two students, who lived in single-parent households, about their anger at not having their fathers in their lives. The first student, a young girl, was being raised by her grandmother, so she carried some extra heavy baggage. She admitted that she had low self-esteem and had questioned her worth because if her own parents didn't want to be a part of her life, who would? Her mother was around sometimes, but she was battling her own demons and couldn't focus as much on her daughter's situation. Her father seldom responded when she reached out to him, so she was "just tired." It was this "just tired" excuse that usually sent her off on wild escapades. She was an honor student with boundless potential; but, like so many other girls whose self-confidence is shaky, she often found herself in icky situations simply because she wanted to feel like she belonged *somewhere*. She started smoking weed, drinking alcohol, and having unprotected sex with multiple boys and grown men. I knew her wild behavior was her way of trying to fill the void her parents' absence left, so I told her they may not realize just how much their absence affected her. Like a lot of relationships, once things ended between the parents, the relationship between parent and child often ended, too. It's as if when the parents stopped seeing each other, at least one parent stopped seeing the child, too. That may not be *right* or *fair*, but more often than not, it is true; so, I told the young girl if she really wanted a relationship with them to just be patient and keep the lines of communication open. She said she would, but we both knew it wouldn't be easy.

The other student, a young boy, admitted it was his father who had tried to build a relationship, but the boy wasn't interested because his father had waited "too long." Like the young girl, his parents hadn't been in a committed relationship when he was conceived, so he was a "casualty of war" so to speak. I never asked Marqus's father if he wanted or was prepared to become a father, and I wasn't going to be forced into a relationship just because my carelessness resulted in an unplanned pregnancy. So, I tried to make my students understand that perhaps the same thing had happened with their parents, but they weren't hearing me. The boy wanted to hate his father, but deep down he knew he didn't. Even though he didn't know the complete history of his parents' relationship, in his eyes, his mother was both mama and daddy, and his father may as well stop trying. His anger was so palpable that I knew it was merely a cover for his pain. As a young boy, he needed the guidance and support of his father but was too stubborn and scared to admit it. He used his father's absence as an excuse to be average even though he was capable of more. After my advice kept falling on deaf ears, I gave up and told him to pray about it because he wasn't as easy to persuade as the young girl.

These students were trying to manage the hurt and anger their parents' absences had inadvertently caused, but they didn't know how to do so. They were looking for someone else, anybody else, to justify their worth because if their own fathers didn't see it, who would? I told them that sometimes we just have to accept that not everybody – including our parents – will make us *feel* worthy. As harsh as that reality seems, it is okay. It's okay because we don't *need* anybody else's validation. We don't *need* anybody else's acceptance. We don't need it, but we do *want* it, and when/if we don't get it, we hurt. That's life, and we have to deal with it. We *can't* control everything that happens to us, but we *can* control how we react/respond to it.

So, regardless what you face in life; regardless what you don't know or don't have; regardless of who is or is not an active part of your life, eliminate the excuses and accept ownership for your own destiny because *nobody* owes us more than we owe ourselves.

Lesson 3: *Keep your circle small*

"When people show you who they are, believe them."

Maya Angelou

At a day and time when children are easily manipulated and exploited, it is especially important to know who you *allow* in your circle. I stress the word allow because we give people permission to be important to us, to be meaningful parts of our lives.

Adolescence, ages 12 to 19, is a time of clarity, a time when a lot of things become clearer. It is the period of independent growth that will ultimately shape you into your *real* self. It is during adolescence when most children start to form and follow their own opinions, tastes, and voices. It is also during this time that independent personalities start to develop, and you recognize not only changes in yourself but in your friends as well. This is the time when you learn to distinguish your supporters from your "haters," the time you recognize the weight of your friends' words and the honesty in their actions. Adolescence is the time when vulnerabilities and jealousies are exposed, and it is during this time when you want the validation and support of your friends the most. The harsh reality, however, is not everybody, including your family and friends, will acknowledge, applaud, or appreciate your growth. A harsher reality is that often your worst enemy, your harshest critic, and your fiercest competitor are those people who are closest to you. Thus, the composition of your circle, i.e. who you invite into your circle, should not be taken lightly.

Many of my students throw the phrase "best

friend" around so loosely and so thoughtlessly that it almost holds no value or significance. What's worse is that many of these students have no idea what a *best* friend is, and even worse, they don't know how to be a *good* friend themselves. They haven't grasped the importance of keeping private things private, and they haven't discerned the difference between an "acquaintance" and a "friend." A lot of these same students come to me complaining about their "best friend" acting "funny" all of a sudden. It may seem as if things changed overnight, but, more than likely, there were obvious signs earlier in the friendship that things were changing. I often tell students they will outgrow people just as they outgrow clothes. Just because they have been friends since kindergarten doesn't mean they will be friends for life. They might, but not all juvenile relationships last a lifetime.

In elementary school, we are led by the influence of other people, usually our parents, because we have not yet developed our own sense of individuality.

By the time we get to upper middle school or early high school, which is also around the time most children become teenagers, we will have a better idea of who we are as an individual. This is when those little differences among friends develop into big problems. This is when we start to see more clearly who is real and who is not. This is also when we start to form our circle. It is important to know who you allow in your circle, but it is more important to know how to separate yourself from people who have proven themselves unworthy of your friendship. The spaces in our circle should be reserved for the people we trust, the ones we believe will have our best interests at heart. Too often, however, these people become the very people who stunt our growth and impede our journey with stumbling blocks. Therefore, we may have to readjust our circles from time to time. Don't get me wrong. I am not suggesting that every person in our circle is distrustful or conniving, but I am saying we have to be the type of friend we want. We have to guard our own business before we expect others to guard it for us. We have to tell and show *only* that which we don't mind being shared with people *outside* our circle because knowing which friend told our business is not as important as knowing what business to share and what business to withhold. I learned this lesson the hard way.

When I was younger, I shared a lot of my personal business with the people in my circle. I told them practically everything. I told them about embarrassing, illicit things I had done, about my financial situation, and even about intimate things I had done with the men I dated. None of that should have been a problem since these where my "peeps," right? Surely nothing I said would be used against me because these people were my *friends*, right? Wrong! Dead wrong!! When other people, some with whom I'd never had any type of real conversation, could discuss my business as if I had been the one who told them (and I knew that I hadn't), I realized that I had to reevaluate the composition of my circle. I had to differentiate *and* separate *acquaintances* from *friends*, and I apparently needed to decrease the circumference of my circle. I'm not sure if they told out of spite or jealousy, or if they really didn't think that their telling someone else would be a problem. What I do know is that they repeated stuff I didn't want repeated, so somebody had to go. How dare they tell my business? Nevertheless, when my initial anger finally subsided, my clarity increased. I had to admit my own fault in the situation. How dare I tell my business? I couldn't be upset with *anyone* in my circle unless I was *more* upset with myself. If *I* hadn't told my business, *nobody* else would've been able to tell it. I had trusted others to keep my business a secret when I hadn't kept it a secret myself.

It's important to surround yourself with people who will be honest with you even if that honesty hurts. You may *want* the people in your circle to agree with everything you say and do, but you *need* people who will support your development and tell you when you're wrong. Your circle should be so intimate that if/when they correct you, you'll know their criticism and honesty come from a place of love and are meant to help, not hurt.

Today, my circle is so small 'til it could be considered a dot. I've weeded out a lot of people, and a lot of people have weeded me out. That's okay. The few people in my circle know and accept the real me, the flawed me. They don't say stuff just because it's what I want to hear or because it'll make me happy. They give me the raw truth even when it stings. I've learned to appreciate their brutal honesty because the truth never needs to be filtered, and it should never come with an apology.

Even though I have welcomed only a few people in my circle, the *most important* part of my circle is God. He has a firsthand view of all my faults and shortcomings, but He never holds them against me. He knows the good, the bad, and the ugly. He knows my deepest fears and my darkest secrets – things I have never shared with any other member of my circle; and He ***still*** loves me. He knows I'm imperfect; He knows I'm still going to mess up; He knows I am not worthy of His goodness; yet, He has never turned His back on me. He's remained right by my side through all my mess. Even today, after all the stuff I've done, after all the mistakes I've made, He simply looks beyond my faults and doesn't just *see* my needs; He *supplies* them. Yes, He chastises me when I'm wrong, and He corrects me when I mess up, but He does it so I can do and be better. So, even though my friends are great, they can't be, they can't give, and they can't do what God can. Don't just take my word for it. Establish your own relationship with God; invite Him to be a part of your circle. I can tell you how awesome He has been to me, but nothing I say will prepare you for your own relationship with Him. He will be just as awesome to you. It doesn't matter that you aren't as old as I am because you're never too young to know Him for yourself!! Even at a young age, you will encounter situations and people that will test you and cause you to question to your worth. That's when God will show you His powers. When people *want* to do you harm, God won't *let* them. He will help you to bend without breaking, to shift without shaking. He will order not only your steps, but the steps of the people in your circle, too. Who wouldn't want a friend like that? So, no matter who else you allow in your circle, be sure to invite God. I promise you won't regret that you did.

STACY L. MOORE

Lesson 4: *Everybody make mistakes; don't let yours define you.*

"Hey, I'ma make mistakes in life/Yes sir/I'm not perfect, ya heard me? (I'm not perfect)/

You know, don't judge me..."

Kevin Gates "In God I Trust"

Making mistakes, even the careless, embarrassing ones, is an inevitable part of life; and, contrary to popular belief, these types of mistakes are *not* exclusive to adolescents. Even as an experienced adult, I still make stupid mistakes, but I don't allow those mistakes to hold me hostage, and I don't let them define me.

I was fairly withdrawn as a teen, and even though my parents worked hard to make sure my siblings and I were "good" kids, I still strayed. When I left home for college, I was an innocent virgin, who was destined for academic excellence. After just a few months of uncontrolled freedom, I had become the complete opposite. I did things just because I could. I went to clubs, hung out all night, and smoke and drank 'til I got tired. I'd had sex with a few guys that led absolutely nowhere, but I wasn't even fazed by that fact because I wanted to catch up on all the fun my dad hadn't allowed me to have. I was living my best life, and my dad would *never* know. Then, I got pregnant. That stopped everything because now my dad *would* know, and he wouldn't be happy. Because I never wanted to disappoint my dad, I lied about my son's paternity. I figured if he didn't know who my son's father was, he would accept my pregnancy easier. I told them the father was this contractor from New York, who had worked at Tougaloo for a few months. I figured the guy was so far away that I would be able to raise my son alone. To say that lie backfired is a gross understatement. The guy wanted to be involved in Marqus's life, which posed more problems than it was worth. He came to Mississippi to "meet" Marqus, so I was forced to come clean and notify the *real* father, which wasn't as bad as I had thought it would be. Though my deception did not destroy Marqus's relationship with his dad *or* my relationship with mine, that one mistake *could* have had lasting consequences. Even now, over 26 years later, when somebody tries to remind me of my mistake, I smile and change the subject because I will not allow that mistake, or the thousand others I've made, to tarnish my present; and I absolutely refuse to let anybody make me an emotional hostage because of my past. I did it, it's done, and it won't *ever* be undone. Case closed – *permanently* – so save your judgment.

When I was a teenager, there was no social media, and cell phones were not as widespread as they are now. The only way my generation got "exposed" was by word of mouth. People talked about each other's business, but there were no pictures or videos to prove or disprove what was said. Today, however, it takes only seconds to spread information, and often there *is* irrefutable proof like pictures and audio and video recordings to substantiate that information. Since the influx of social media, people from all walks of life have been caught on candid camera – often in embarrassing situations. The worst part is that many times those unflattering situations are posted on social media *without* the victim's knowledge or consent. Contrary to what teens and young adults seem to believe, social media is nobody's friend. Once things are posted, it is virtually impossible to control what happens to them.

Many young girls have been "exposed" on social media by an irate ex-boyfriend, a jealous friend, or a vicious enemy, and such negative attention has left these girls open to constant attacks from others. Unfortunately, I've encountered quite a few young girls who have been caught in this type of situation, and I've seen the crippling effects of other people's negativity on these girls. Case in point: A few years ago, lewd pictures of a young girl circulated on social media and throughout the school.

Naturally, the girl was embarrassed, but worse than that, she felt hopeless. After the pictures were leaked, she returned to school where several of her peers taunted her, and everywhere she went, somebody was snickering or whispering. She'd been sent to the office for cursing students and disrupting class after students kept teasing her about the pictures. When I saw her looking dejected and lost, my heart ached for her. Although I wasn't her teacher, I pulled her to the side, and she shamefully admitted she had sent the pictures to her "boyfriend" because he'd said he missed her and having a picture of her would make him feel better. After she sent the pictures, he asked her to make a video *with* him *and* his friends. When she refused, he posted the risqué pictures on social media. He was a few years older than she and could have faced criminal charges, but the girl didn't like the possibility of even more people knowing about her mistake. After I was finally able to convince her that the pictures were not the end of the world, I told her people would continue to taunt her until she reclaimed control of the situation. She asked how she could do that, and the advice I gave her is the same advice I would have given my goddaughter if she had put herself in such a position. I said, "The next time somebody mentions the pictures, ask them if you were cute. Ask them if they noticed your new hairdo. Ask them if you looked happy. Ask them *anything* because they won't be expecting it." She was shocked! Good!! If I had shocked her, she would stun her perpetrators, and they would eventually leave her alone. I told her that I hoped she'd learned an important lesson so she wouldn't allow herself to be in that position again. She assured me she had and thanked me for my advice. When she left the counselor's office, she knew people would still talk about the incident, but she was in a better headspace to begin coping with it. I'm not trivializing the situation or condoning the irrational behavior, but I understood her dilemma. She's young and gullible, and she wanted to make her boyfriend happy. She's not the only woman who's ever been that crazy in love, and she won't be the last. She had already beaten herself up about the situation, so why should she give others permission to punish her when some of them had made worse mistakes themselves? As devastating as it was, she should simply consider that embarrassing mistake a lesson learned and try not to make the same mistake again.

People will try to hold your past over your head for as long as they can. They will act as if what you did is the worst thing ever although many of them have done things that were far worse. You can do a million great things and make one mistake, and people will likely remember that one mistake longer than they will the million great things. When I was in high school, one of my classmates was caught having sex in the restroom with three or four boys. Her parents were called to the school, and she was suspended. When she returned to school a few weeks later, people kept reminding her of her mistake, but she ignored them. After that embarrassment, she somehow managed to turn things around. She stopped skipping class and started doing her work so she could graduate on time. Years later, during a class gathering, several of us were standing around reminiscing when the woman walked in. Like a lot of us, she had aged and gained weight, so she looked different. Somebody asked, "Who is that?" The response was, "That's _____." When the person still looked confused, a guy said, "You remember her. She's the girl they caught having sex in the restroom that time..." That jarred the other guy's memory and eventually led to them recalling more sordid memories. Not once did anybody, not even me, mention the way the girl had turned her life around or how she had become one of the most successful people in our class. They were simply content to dwell on the negative as if that had been her life-defining moment. So, if you've been "exposed" or made any other embarrassing mistake, the best thing you can do for yourself is get over it. People have already heard about or seen it, and *nothing* you do will make them un-hear or un-see it, so stop beating yourself up about it. Own your mistake, so it doesn't own you. As long as people think their opinions *of* you matter *to* you, they will never relinquish that sense of control. There's no need trying to convince people they are right or wrong about you because once you start, they won't let you stop; and they will *still* form their own opinions. Don't let *any* mistake hold you hostage. Forgive yourself – even if no one else will, so that you don't become emotionally paralyzed and\or indefinitely traumatized. Don't let your present be clouded by your past; and although your past will indeed shape your present, it doesn't have to control your future.

STACY L. MOORE

.

Lesson 5: *Don't allow others to use you.*

This lesson is the "rawest" because there is no gentle way to speak candidly about sex among teens.

"But you didn't have to cut me off/Make out like it never happened and that we were nothing
And I don't even need your love/But you treat me like a stranger and that feels so rough…"

Goyte "Somebody I Used to Know"

In a world where so much emphasis is placed on the *idea* of perfection, it is not surprising that many girls have low self-esteem. Often, because of low self-esteem, many of these girls haven't realized they are worthy. They want to feel like they belong *somewhere,* so they allow themselves to be used, to be treated like either throwaway conveniences or community property –specifically by boys. (Throwaway conveniences are the cheap stuff like paper plates and cups that can be thrown away *immediately* after use. Community property is any insignificant thing that is passed from person to person and is often used by many but claimed by none.) Boys can sense girls' insecurities, and they pounce on them with little or no regard for the girls' feelings. Sadly, by the time many young girls become adults, they will have many insecurities and even more sexual partners– all before they realize that their worth does not lie within the juncture between their thighs.

Sex is a game-changer – even for adults, so it stands to reason that for teens, it is even more profound. Sex causes irrevocable changes within the body and mind, so the younger a person is when he or she becomes sexually active, the worse the damage can be. Sex doesn't just escalate physical development;

it also awakens a sense of mental and emotional awareness, which can open that proverbial can of worms that can easily multiply into a sea of carelessness among children.

When I was younger, most girls didn't become sexually active until high school. I started even later than that. I didn't lose my virginity until I was in college. Today, however, girls are persuaded to engage in sex as early as upper elementary school, and with the advent of social media, it is much easier for kids to scheme and schedule trysts ("hookups") without their parents' knowledge. It may seem crazy to think that innocent nine- and ten-year old kids even know what sex is, but they do. They see it virtually everywhere, so, naturally, they become curious. They use their cell phones and other gadgets to investigate these curiosities. They use Google and Siri to find more than games and YouTube videos. Case in point: A few years ago, several elementary school students, all girls, were caught in the bathroom watching adult videos. They were on a bathroom break, but when it took them longer than usual to return, the teacher went to get them. She found them huddled in a group watching the lewd videos on a cell phone. What an eye-opening experience that was for the teachers, parents, and school administrators!! It shocked them, but it also made them more aware. It caused the adults to reevaluate sex education in school and at home.

Although sex isn't as taboo today as it was when I was a child, a lot of parents still tend to avoid the "big talk" until they (the parents themselves) are ready. As parents, we don't always consider our children's readiness because we want them to stay our babies for as long as they can. It is this avoidance on our part that multiplies our children's uncertainties and leaves them to discover sex on their own, which can lead to some pretty scary situations. If your parents trust you enough to let you go places with your friends or do things with your boyfriend, don't abuse that trust. If you think you are ready for sex or if you are simply curious about it, go to your parents. Allow them the opportunity to answer your questions before you listen to your friends or someone else. When Marqus came to me about sex, I was nervous and shocked. Why did he grow up before I was ready? As tough as I thought I was, sex was a scary topic for me to discuss with my teenage son. Since he was honest enough to come to me, though, I had to be as open and honest with him. He asked questions that made my hair stand on end, but I had to tell him the truth. He needed to know that a few moments of pleasure could cost him a lifetime of pain. He had to understand that having unprotected sex was an open invitation to handcuff himself to a girl for the rest of his life – even if he didn't know or like her for more than her body. I needed him to understand that it didn't take but one pump and a swirl to get a baby or a disease, and I needed him to understand that not all diseases are curable with a shot or a pill. When he asked what he was supposed to do if she said he could "go in raw," I almost swallowed my tongue. I was dumbfounded that my 14-year-old son would use such language, but I had to boss up and keep it real. I told him not to consider himself special if she told him that because she had probably allowed other boys to "go in raw," too. I told him that meant he would also be going in "raw" with everybody she'd had sex with. He didn't like that idea, but I still have three grandbabies, so he must've ignored my advice at least three times. (That's a story for another time, though.) By the time we finished "the talk," he was almost too scared to try it. Of course, he eventually did, but he had a better idea about some of the consequences and dangers that lurk behind a cute face and a nice body.

Sex among teens is scary because so many teenagers seem to think they are *supposed* to engage in sex as often as possible with as many partners as possible. Because they are young, they think they're *supposed* to "live their best life." They don't think they should worry about anything but having fun, so a lot of them seldom stop long enough to consider risky consequences like tarnished reputations, unwanted pregnancies, and sexually transmitted diseases. Case in point: Not long ago, I spoke with a young girl who had been caught performing oral sex on several boys at school. That a girl her age (she was barely 14 at the time) even knew what oral sex was, let alone was willing to *do* it, was beyond incredulous to me! After word spread about her antics, children around the school started teasing her and calling her vulgar names. If that wasn't bad enough, boys started stopping her in the hall during the change of classes trying to give her money. I had no idea what the boys were doing until I overheard her classmates talking about it. Apparently she had "charged" the boys a small fee for her "services," and several other boys wanted to cash in on the "sale." When the students kept teasing her, I pulled her to the side and tried to talk to her. She claimed she wasn't bothered by the negative attention, but I could see in her face that she was. Who wouldn't be? I felt helpless and embarrassed for her, but she seemed dazed by the whole thing. It was as if she didn't fully grasp the magnitude of her actions. Her body had developed much faster than her mind. I asked her why she did it, and she just shrugged her shoulders and said one of the boys asked and when she "did" him, he told other boys and they wanted it, so it just "grew from there." She had done grown-up things, but she sounded more like a lost toddler than a teenaged high school student. Those boys had taken advantage of her inexperience and used her for their enjoyment, but she didn't know how to stop them. When I asked why she let the boys just throw money at her, she seemed offended by my question. It was as if she thought she had "earned" the money even though it came with total disregard for her feelings. I told her boys would use her as long as she allowed them to, and not even a million dollars would be enough to buy her some self-respect. Then she admitted that she had gone even farther with some of the boys (yes, at school), and they had not used protection. I was floored! I tried to reason with her, but she seemed more interested in her newfound popularity than she was in anything I said. I could tell my words were missing their mark, so I just told her if she ever wanted to talk, we could. When she left, I felt as if I had failed not only her but myself as well. Chances are her reputation will be permanently scarred by that one incident even though she wasn't mature enough to grasp the full extent of her actions.

Not long after that, one of my male students came to me because he thought one of his "pieces" might be pregnant. Though he claimed to be "worried," he was nonchalant as he talked about the situation. I asked what his plans were if the girl really was pregnant. He said he would simply say the baby wasn't his since some of his "boys" had had sex with her, too. Shocked, I asked why he wasn't bothered by the fact that he and his friends had had sex with the same girl. His response has left an indelible mark on my psyche, and even today, I remember his retort – verbatim. He said, "Man…we family. Everybody [gone] eat." He bragged about how he had "put my boys on her" because she wasn't his "main woman…she was just something to do." Even as I write those words, I am *still* floored by the off-handed way he spoke of this girl and his sex-capades because at the time he was only 15 years old, and the girl was even younger. He said that *all* he had to do was "slide in" one of her social media posts, and it was "easy from there." He said the girl did all the work after that. She convinced her mom she needed to stay after school one day to make up some work for class, and she "just hung out" until he was finished with football practice. He said he "hit" her in the back seat of his friend's car while his friend drove them around. I was dumbfounded, but he wasn't finished. He said she texted him later that night, but he didn't respond. He showed me some of the messages, and I was embarrassed for her because she was literally begging him for attention. When he finally responded, he was rude and showed no regard for her feelings. Still, she kept texting him. He laughed because she thought they were "together" after the "hook-up," but once he'd gotten what he wanted, he said he was done. When I asked what he'd do if she was pregnant, he said, "Oh, well. That'll be on her and her mama." I was dumbfounded -- again. He didn't really want advice; he simply wanted to brag about his conquest. It was obvious that he was not affected by the thought that she could be pregnant because, for him, it had been nothing more than sex. He was prepared to do grown-up things but not prepared for grown-up consequences. Luckily, she wasn't pregnant, but I don't think she really thought she was; she just wanted to hold on to the boy. He'd treated her as if she were simply an insignificant pawn in a low-stakes game of checkers that could be easily discarded without any concern for her feelings or her safety. He had used her and then treated her like a throwaway convenience, but she had allowed it.

That incident could have resulted in an unwanted pregnancy, but pregnancy isn't the only risky consequence of casual sex among irresponsible teens. The more sexual partners a person has, especially if the sex is unprotected, the more chances for sexually transmitted diseases. A lot of young girls are not on any type of birth control because they are too scared to tell their parents they are sexually active. Even still, they don't force the boys to wear condoms. The girls admit they want the boys to use protection, but when the boys say it "won't feel the same," the girls "just give in" because they "don't want to lose" the boys. It doesn't help much when I remind the girls that without protection, they are giving the boys permission to poison their bodies with anything the boys' other sexual partners may have had. What if one of the other girls had a disease? What if the boy is bisexual?

The girls may look scared and may even think about my questions, but they still don't force the boys to wear condoms. Case in point: A girl came to me distraught and embarrassed because her "boyfriend" had shunned her after they had had sex. She was slightly overweight and couldn't afford name brand clothes or the long weave and eyelashes that many of her classmates wore, so she was flattered by this jock's attention. She said he'd "hit me up on Snapchat" and asked to "hook up," but they had never actually talked to each other – not even on the day they had unprotected sex in his friend's car. (Do kids ever have sex anywhere else, or is everybody just "doing it" in cars nowadays?) When she saw him at school after the "hook-up," he avoided her. Still, she kept following him until he finally embarrassed her in front of her friends. He told her he didn't want her and she was "just a piece of ___!" She was devastated but still unwilling to accept his rejection. She said, "He just said that so his girlfriend wouldn't find out." In her mind, they were "together," so even after he dissed her in front of her friends, whenever he wanted to sex her, she let him. A few weeks into the "relationship," his friends started trying to "holler at" her. She was really flattered because some of his friends were "cuter than him." Since he refused to dump his girlfriend for her, she figured she'd "pay him back by sleeping with his friends." Thinking she'd make him jealous, she sent him screenshots of the messages his friends had sent her. To her utter embarrassment, he responded by sending several laughing emojis. When she asked him what that meant, he said he didn't care who or what she did. Soon after that she learned that her "boyfriend" had been the one who *recommended* her to his friends. He had been the one to tell them she was "easy and freaky." She was really embarrassed when they told her they wanted her to "do" them like she'd "done" their "boy." The worst part is she had already had sex (yes, unprotected) with some of his friends before she learned it was just a game to them. All of them had treated her like community property, and there was not much she could do about it since she'd willingly put herself in such a damaging position. Although I felt bad for her, I felt obligated to keep it real. She knew the boy already had a girlfriend when he texted her, yet she still accepted his *invitation*. I told her that since he never insinuated that he was ending his previous relationship to begin one with her, she should have read the fine print on his contract before she signed on his dotted line. If she had been honest about what all of those boys really wanted from her *before* she'd had sex with them, she probably could've saved herself a lot of embarrassment. She was angry with the boys, but she really should have been angry with herself. They had not forced themselves on her, and they had not forced her to *give* herself to them. She wanted me to validate her behavior and tell her she was right, but I couldn't do that. I suggested she talk with her mother about birth control and STD's because she wasn't sure if she had contracted anything from them or not. She had willingly put herself in a position to let others use her, so she had to deal with the consequences. She wasn't exactly happy about my advice, but she did recognize the honesty in it. Hopefully, she won't allow herself to be used like that again.

As I thought about the insecure and naïve young girls, who are so easily duped by boys, I wanted to cry! These girls were swimming in a sea of promiscuity and didn't even realize they needed a life jacket. I was speechless, and I felt helpless. *How* could I impact these girls *en masse*? I wanted to be their life jacket and save them from their self-destructive behaviors, but I knew I couldn't. It's like the adage says, "You can take a horse to the water, but you can't make it drink." These girls would have to *want* to save themselves before I or anybody else could help them.

Not long after my conversation with that young lady, I overheard a group of male students discussing their recent sex-capades. That they were even sexually active at 14 and 15 years old still makes me cringe, but what they said was even more startling. All of them claimed to have more than one "girl," and each "girl" had a "job." They had labeled the girls as either the "Boo," the "Side-boo," the "Hook-up," or the "Go-to." My curiosity was peaked, so I asked what makes the girls different. How do they know which girl gets which "job"? They spoke as candidly with me as they had with each other and ended up teaching me a lesson I will never forget. They told me they categorize the girls simply by observing them "in action." They said they usually watch the girl for a few days before they approach her, so they know beforehand which "job" she'll get. I was shocked, but I'd gone too far to stop. I asked them to explain each "job," and they were more than happy to oblige.

The "Boo" is the main girl; she's the "boss," the

"wifey." Her position is the most coveted, but the least filled. They said, "She makes you work for it," so she is the one who is seen with him in public, the one who is introduced to his family, and the one who is lavished with gifts. She is also "protected" by the boy's friends and is off-limits for any kind of disrespect. The "Boo" can talk to the boy's friends because they won't tell her anything that'll hurt her, even if that means they have to lie to her. Her feelings matter. It's an unspoken rule that she is kept out of harm's way, especially from his other girls, and she's never to be treated like community property – even after a breakup. The "Boo" is the *most* special of all the girls.

The "Side-boo" is not as high up as the "Boo," but her perks are *almost* as comparable. The "Side-boo" *could* be the "Boo" if there wasn't one already. She *may* get to introduce the boy to *her* family, but *if* she is introduced to his family, it is usually as "a friend." She *may* be seen in public with him, but *never* in places where he and the "Boo" go. The "Side-boo" is moderately respected by his friends, but not to the extent the "Boo" is. The boys tolerate her, but she is not "protected" like the "Boo" is. The "Side-boo" is *not* off-limits and *can* be pursued by the other crew members. Because she is not as special as the "Boo," the "Side-boo" *could* become community property.

The "Hook-up" is only in the picture for those times when the "Boo" and the "Side-boo" are "tripping" or unavailable. The "Hook-up" won't likely be seen in public as she seldom requires more than a text message or social media "like" to request her time. His friends give her absolutely no respect since she and her antics are often discussed among the boys to see how many of them are also interested in her time. She's not special for anything beyond the time the boy allows her to be in his presence.

The "Go-to" is there for those times when the boy wants a "quickie." She offers little resistance, so she may be visited more than the other three girls, but she is the least respected. She seldom requires any kind of invitation, so the boy is allowed to "go to" her for his pleasure whenever he chooses. Just like the "Hook-up," she gets absolutely no respect from him or his boys, and she, too, is *recommended* to his boys. She's special only in her mind and is quickly forgotten until her services are needed again.

As I listened to the boys discuss this phenomenon, I tried not to be repulsed, but I was indeed appalled by the number of girls who willingly accept being the "Hook-up" or the "Go-to." These girls are so thirsty for attention and validation that they knowingly allow themselves to be used. They should know exactly what the boy is seeking or offering *before* they give themselves to him. As females, we can't be afraid to ask males what it is they *really* want because we do have the right to decline their offers. In the boys' defense, though, if/when we don't ask, we can't be mad or disappointed when we get what we didn't want or expect. Chances are if he already has a "Boo" or even a "Side-boo," he is not offering that position because if he wanted you for one of those spots, he'd make sure it was available *before* he approached you. Furthermore, according to the boys, the "Side-boo," "Hook-up," and "Go-to" almost never get "upgraded" from their initial positions. They either keep the original position or "get fired if they start complaining too much." In other words, if the boy was able to get what he wanted without offering a contract, he's not likely to offer one after he's gotten what he wanted.

Males won't treat you any better than you treat yourself, and they will only treat you the way you allow them to. If you act like a fast-food restaurant, they will simply make a quick stop at your drive-thru window, collect their order, and leave. Similarly, if you act like an all-you-can-eat buffet, where you get more food for a discounted price, men will simply sup at your table, go back as many trips as they want, wait, belch, and repeat.

Once they've gotten their fill, they will leave and let you clean up mess. If a boy *and* his friends can get your goodies with minimal output, they will. They won't expend any more effort or energy than you require. Therefore, you have to demand to be treated like you are worth more than a "4-for-4".

You have to learn how to become an upscale, fine-dining establishment where the patrons double check themselves before they cross your threshold. You have to demand a *shirt-and-tie* type atmosphere where you post a sign that says you "reserve the right to refuse service" if a patron doesn't fulfill your requirements. You have to demand respect – without explanation or apology!

If you demand such courtesy from males, however, you must demand just as much of yourselves. This means you must hold yourselves to the same (or higher) standards that you expect from the males. If you want the males to be of a certain caliber before they can even *think* about dining at your restaurants, you have to make sure everything – from the outer appearance to the inner ambience – is top-notch. This means you have to take pride in your appearance *and* in your hygiene. You have to make sure you look *and* smell your best at all times because you never know when you may be called to host an exquisite party. I can't tell you how many times in the past 20 years I've heard boys diss girls for bad body odors. Yes, the boys *still* "did" the girls, but they almost always made the girls the brunt of jokes – sometimes in the girls' presence – after the boys had gotten what they wanted. This is why personal hygiene is so important. When I was in school, we had Home Economics classes where personal hygiene was a major component. We were taught how to use feminine products like pads and tampons. We learned the benefits and dangers of intimate deodorant products like douches and feminine washes. Nowadays, however, young girls don't have Home Economic classes, and many of them are scared to ask questions, so they just make it up as they go along. A lot of people say if they are old enough to be having sex, they ought to be old enough to know how to wash themselves properly, but this is not always the case. Young girls have to be taught that cleanliness is a daily obligation that will likely *need* to increase once they become sexually active. They have to be taught that if they still have an odor after washing with soap and water, they may need to try some of the other products like douches or feminine washes that are designed specifically for intimate female hygiene. If they don't know how to use these products, they should find a woman they trust and ask her to show them because no woman wants a bad odor to be her legacy.

In our Home Economics classes we were also taught that the way we dress can affect how people view us.

Young girls today seem to think the less they have on, the more a boy will want them; and to an extent, they are right. The boy may want what the girls seem to be advertising, but he may not want anything beyond that. Getting a boy's attention is easy, but keeping it requires a little more work. The way you dress may also affect the caliber of boys you attract. If you flaunt all of your goodies and put your whole self on display, boys can assume that all you're looking for is a "booty call," and they'll think they can treat you like a throwaway convenience. If you present yourself in a more modest way where they simply get a hint of your goodies, you'll make them work hard to earn you.

They'll respect you because you respect yourself. Before you get offended, I'm not saying there is anything wrong with being proud of your figure. However, I am saying you can't be upset when people perceive you the way you present you. There's an old saying, "If it looks like a duck and sounds like a duck, then it must be a duck." So, boys may think, "If she's dressed like a _____ and looks like a _____, then she must be a _____." So, you have to decide which "job" you want. If you want to be his "Boo" or "Side-boo," you have to make him earn you and your goodies. On the other hand, if you're ok with being the "Hook-up" or the "Go-to," feel free to put all your goodies on display and don't worry about consequences. The choice is all yours, not his!

As females, we must set our standards high and force males to *try* to reach our levels. When we want them to stop categorizing us based solely on their opinions, we will make sure that our actions will get us the results we want. *You* have to believe you deserve more than a quick *ride* in the back seat of a car; *you* have to know you are worth more than a pump and swirl before you can expect boys to treat you as if they know it. In other words, if/when we start acting as if we know our worth is not connected to our vaginas, men will do the same.

Lesson 6: *Don't lose you trying to keep him.*

This lesson was the toughest to write because, in an effort to be as truthful as I'm asking you to be, I had to expose my vulnerabilities and awaken demons I had laid to rest years ago. I had to resurrect unpleasant memories and put them on display even though leaving them buried would have been much easier. However, not facing these demons would have defeated my purpose for writing this book. So, here goes!!!

"Oh, what a feeling/The one that I thought that I needed
Was incapable of needing me back/
Incapable of loving like that/Mmm incapable..."

Keyshia Cole "Incapable

"

"Gave you all I had and you tossed it in the trash.../
You know I'd do anything for ya/I would go through all this

pain.../
But you won't do the same"

Bruno Mars "Grenade"

I am the sum total of *every* man that I ever allowed to touch me, be that touch physical or emotional, and it all started with my dad. My dad is the measuring stick by which all other men are measured. He was my first example of what a real man should be, and even today, I judge every man I date by the standards he set. I don't do this on purpose, but it's an involuntary habit I have noticed over the past few years. My dad is strong – both physically and mentally. He is handsome, independent, a tad bit arrogant, and extremely unemotional. So, I generally migrate to men with similar characteristics. My dad never met a challenge he hated. He believes if it has ever been done by any human, surely, he can do it, too. I get my drive and tenacity from my dad, so a lot of men – including my dad – think I am a handful. Virtually *every* man I ever dated wanted to "break" me. They wanted to control me, but the harder they worked to manage me, the harder I worked to ensure they *never* would.

I've heard a lot of men use the excuse, "My dad wasn't around to show me how to be a man..." or "I didn't have my father around to show me how to treat a woman..." I've also heard a lot of women use similar excuses: "My mom didn't show me how to be a woman," or "I didn't grow up with my dad in my life, so I didn't have anybody around to show me how a man was supposed to treat a woman." My dad was more involved in my development as a woman than my mother was, so I can't use those same excuses, *but* I *still* wrestled with some of those same issues. I can't recall seeing any lasting examples of healthy, happy relationships during my teen years. I did witness a lot of relationships, but most of them were toxic or unhealthy. Some of them were physically abusive, but most of them were emotionally abusive. So, I guess my enduring and overcoming an emotionally abusive relationship was my rite of passage so to speak.

Even with my dad being a big part of my emotional maturation, I still let men treat me like dirt. Even after having such a great model for what a man should be, I still let men treat me like I wasn't worthy. So, the excuses about having someone in your life to show you how to be a woman or how a man should treat you are all pointless. No matter who is or who is not an active part of our lives, at some point, we have to become accountable for our own actions, and blaming other people for our screw-ups isn't fair to them or us. We, not the other people, make the mistakes. We make the bad judgment calls, so we have to accept responsibility for those mess-ups and work harder to not keep making them.

Like a lot of my students, when I finally got a little freedom from my dad (in college), I went boy-crazy. I wanted to be wanted, and since I was so inexperienced and naïve, boys found me an easy prey. It was as if they could smell my innocence as soon as I entered a room, and they pounced on it like a cat does a mouse. They used and abused my innocence, but I wasn't totally blameless. They did to me only what I allowed. As I said in Lesson 1, college was my doorway to freedom. I could go places and do things freely without having to worry about my dad finding out. Like a lot of young girls, I thought my worth was dictated by how many boys wanted me, so I allowed myself to be used because I figured if men wanted me, surely I was worth *something*. When Marqus was younger, I could hide behind him and say I didn't have time for a man; but when Marqus got older and jumped out of the nest, I had to find something to do with myself. Sadly, that something almost always involved a man who wasn't worth the effort. The really sad part is I usually didn't *admit* he wasn't worth the effort until I had already given myself to him.

After years of going-nowhere relationships, I had to admit that all of those men couldn't be the problem; after all I was the common denominator among them. So, I took a long, honest look in the mirror, and I finally understood why many of them never recognized or honored my worth – at least not beyond the bedroom. They treated me just as I treated myself – like a piece of worth*less*, damaged meat. They found me interesting enough – likely because of my body, but they seldom bothered to know *me*. We never went out in public – no movies, dinner, or dancing. We never visited other couples. We never went on long walks outside or other stuff like that. Honestly, we seldom went anywhere except the bedroom, and I didn't complain about it. I simply accepted what they offered even if/when I wanted more. It wasn't until a heart-to-heart conversation with Marqus and my goddaughter DeAundra that I had to stop trying to outrun my insecurities. We were discussing the upcoming birth of my first grandchild, and I was fussing at Marqus, who was barely 20 at the time, about responsibility and living too fast. Somehow they turned the tables, and the talk became about me and marriage. I said the only way I could be married was if my husband and I kept separate homes. I laughed. They didn't. DeAundra asked me *why* I didn't want to be married, and I said I didn't "want to be bothered." The truth was I didn't think I was *worthy* enough to be a wife. A lot of my past relationships had been with married men. I'm not boasting about that fact, but it is a fact that cannot be undone, so save your judgment and scorn. Some of my friends also *dated* married men, and we used to joke that married men were *safe* because we knew up front where we stood. We knew up front that we would not be first in their lives, and we pretended to be okay with that. In all honesty I chose married men because I didn't feel worthy of my own monogamous relationship since I had been on the wrong side of marriage for so long. Again, save your judgment! This is my truth, and I couldn't have gotten to this point of clarity or growth without having gone through these things. Everybody has a past, and I own mine because I won't let it own me.

As I've said before, I *dated* married men for years, and I don't remember exactly what caused my awakening or when it really happened, but one day, I just got tired. I got tired of living on a man's time and settling for only the little bit of himself he offered. I got tired of him having time for sex but no time for much else. I got tired of putting his wants before my needs. So, I stopped allowing myself to be used. It wasn't easy, and it didn't happen overnight, but I did finally break the cycle of self-destruction that had lasted for so many years. During this period of renewal and re-invention, I focused on me – mind, body, and soul. I made a conscious decision to love myself, flaws and all, before I tried to love anybody else or before I asked anybody else to love me. I didn't all of a sudden become saved, sanctified, and filled with The Holy Ghost, but I did make time for church. I also made the time to court myself. I took myself on dates. I went to the movies and out to eat all by myself, and I loved it. Marqus always suggested I invite my sister or a cousin because he assumed that I was alone because I *had* to be. I think he secretly felt sorry for me, but I assured him I was alone by choice, not by force. The more time I spent getting to know me, the more time I wanted to spend with me. I was alone, but I was far from lonely. It was during these dates with myself that I learned what I did and didn't want, what I would and would not accept. I swore that no man would ever make the mistake of thinking he *completed* me – as if I were *incomplete* without him. I have always been a whole person. I may have been flawed and tattered at times, but I have always been a *complete* whole *all* by myself. I made sure I could take care of myself physically, emotionally, and financially. So, if/when a man decided he had had enough and wanted to leave, I wouldn't be lost. I might miss his presence, but I wouldn't lose *anything* I needed. I swore that by the time I allowed another man to be part of my life, he would be in for the ride of his life. Never in my wildest dreams did I think *I* would be the one on the ride of a lifetime, especially so soon after my emotional transformation, but that's exactly what happened.

As I said earlier, I generally migrate to men like my dad, and the man who inspired *this* lesson was more like my dad than *all* of the other men I had ever *dated*. I had learned a lot about myself during my self-renewal phase, but I still wasn't prepared for the emotional rollercoaster ride this man took me on. To this day, some five years later, I still can't believe I almost lost me, (yes, the *new* me) trying to keep him.

Let me preface this part by admitting that I knew when we started the *"relationship"* that he was married, but that fact didn't bother me. Again, save your judgment!! This is my truth, and although I'm not proud of *some* of it, I own *all* of it!!I *never* had any desire for him to leave home for me, and I *never* wanted him all to myself – not even after I developed deep feelings for him!!Plus, I knew God would *never* give me what legally belonged to another woman. So, yeah, I knew it was wrong, but I still continued seeing him. That's another story for another time though.

Somewhere within the three years I *dated* this man, I morphed into a woman even I didn't recognize. I became needy and emotional, weak and compliant. I lost the spunk and spark that were part of my DNA. It was as if I had lost all of my senses. I spent more time, effort, and money on this man than all of the other men I ever dated combined. Why? I'm glad you asked. As I said in Lesson 1, I am not what many people call beautiful. On a good day, I may be called cute. I've always known I'm no beauty queen, but I'm no ugly duckling either. I fall somewhere in the middle. So, when this extremely handsome man showed interest in me, I was beyond flattered. It's not that I had never dated handsome men before, but this man was the kind of handsome that stays in your mind long after he's left your presence. I had caught his attention, and I wanted to keep it. I did things for him because, subconsciously, I didn't think I, alone, would be enough to hold his interest for long.

This man was almost a carbon copy of my dad, so I felt safe with him. We could talk for hours at a time about any and every thing without getting bored. He could light up my whole day with just a simple text message. We could finish each other's thoughts with ease, and we could be in each other's company for hours and still not want to leave. You're probably wondering if he was *that* great, why are we not still *together*. After three years of giving, doing, and being whatever I thought this man *could* want or need, I awakened one day to the realization that I was the only one who was giving, doing, and being while he was the only one receiving. Don't get me wrong; he did *say* quite a few times that the relationship wasn't fair to me and he felt "bad" because I was always doing so much for him when he *couldn't* do as much for me. He felt "guilty" because I was so "faithful" to him when he was married to someone one. He even said he'd thought about letting me go a few times, but every time he got ready to do it, he'd get "selfish and say, 'What about me? Who will I have?'" The sad truth is hearing him say that made me *so* happy – until a few months later when I realized he wasn't keeping me around because he had developed feelings for me; he simply wanted me around to fulfill *his* wants/needs. More than once he said he'd "have to do better" because I deserved more than what he was giving. That's what he said, and although he had good intentions, it never really happened; and I never complained. I was the perfect "Side-boo." I never asked him for money. I didn't complain about the amount of time he gave me. I never threw my bills in his face, and I was faithful to him as if he really was *my* man. If another man approached me, I quickly told him I was "seeing somebody." If he asked if it was serious, I'd say, "Very." Still, in spite of having the perfect "Side-boo," this man refused to give me the *one* thing I craved. It wasn't that he *couldn't* give it (because I *never* would have asked for something he *couldn't* give); he just made a *conscious* decision *not* to give it. Like my dad, this man was extremely unaffectionate, but that wasn't an issue because I'm not the cuddling, holding-hands type myself. Still, I wanted *my* man to make me *feel* wanted-- at least once in a while. I *needed* him to show interest in me, not just my body. So, the *one* thing I told this man I needed, the one thing I *begged* this man for was *occasional* compliments -- just to affirm his interest in me. Although I am no beauty queen, I never *had* to ask a man for compliments. I had never had to *beg* a man for confirmation or validation, but with this guy --the one I had done the most for --I did!! It was as if the more he knew I wanted/needed it, the more he was determined to withhold it; the more he withheld it, the harder I worked to make myself indispensable to him. Even when I dressed up for this man (I'm talking stilettos, mini dresses, fishnet stockings, negligees, etc.), he *never* acted as if he even saw it. Then, if I asked if he noticed my outfits, he'd get upset. He never celebrated holidays or special occasions like my birthday or our "anniversary," but I always celebrated his; and any time he expressed interest in something, I got it for him before he could get it for himself. He always accepted my gifts, but he never returned the gesture; and I *still* didn't complain. (He did give me a couple hundred dollars over the three-year period, but it was usually after I'd done something for him, so it felt more like a reimbursement than a gift.) In the three years we *dated,* he *always* "forgot" my birthday even after I'd give hints a few days in advance; and I always hand-delivered him an excuse for it. I'd tell him it was no big deal because I'd had so many birthdays that it wasn't that important; but it was. I just didn't want to push him away by whining or complaining, so I swallowed my hurt and moved forward. In hindsight, I wanted him to *recognize* my worth even though I apparently didn't recognize my own. Yes, that's sad, but it's also true, and this lesson requires complete honesty – even when it exposes my weaknesses.

In his defense, somewhere near the end of our second year, he did *claim* he *wanted* to end things because it "just ain't fair," but I wouldn't *let* him leave me. I told him if I wasn't complaining, then he shouldn't either. I'm sure he expected me to ask him not to leave, so my response was no surprise to him. We continued for another year, with no real effort on his part to truly change, but why *should* he change when all of his needs were being met? Why *should* he give up his comfort – especially since I said I was okay with things as they were? So, after dedicating three whole years to this man, I awakened that day and realized that I was the only one giving, and he was the only one receiving. He had *no* plans to concede on the *one* thing I told him I *needed* even though I was bending over backwards for him. If he could ignore my *one need* so easily, why would I continue trying to meet his *every want*? That realization pissed me off, so I knew our time had finally run its course. I loved him, but my heart would no longer overrule my head. So, when I walked away, it wasn't because I'd suddenly grown a conscience. It wasn't because I'd fallen out of love with him, and it wasn't because I had found something better. It was because I'd grown tired of him not even *trying* to treat me as if I am worthy -- even after all of the things I had endured for him. In short, I got tired of being what he needed but not what he wanted!!Even after I got tired, though, I found myself wondering *how* I would live without this man. *How* could I go on without him as an important part of my life? Then, after a few weeks of crying and second-guessing myself, I realized just how long I had already lived without him. I had lived over 40 years before we even "got together," and I had survived the weeks after we parted; so I knew I *could* survive, and I worked hard to make sure that I would.

I heard a song decades ago that said, "When the heart gives a command, the mind, soul, and body must obey." Apparently it is true because after our "break-up," my sappy heart would lead me to text him just to see if he'd respond. He would, and he'd almost always say something sweet or endearing, which almost always pulled me right back into his cyclone. We'd end up having sex, and afterwards, I'd feel empty and cheap; so, eventually, I stopped texting, and since he seldom initiated contact, I have been able to maintain my decision to leave him alone. On the rare occasions when I do run into him, we speak and keep it moving. No kee-keeing or catching up because there's no need for it. We're done, and I'm better because of it.

I shared this lesson not because I'm proud of it, but because it shows just how resilient our hearts are – especially when they're fueled by determination. After *everything* I had overcome before I dated this man, I *still* almost lost me trying to keep him. Even after years of rehabilitating myself, I *still* almost forgot my own worth in an effort to overcompensate for his. I had *let* him be so important to me for so long that even I didn't think I had the emotional fortitude to walk away from him for good. Had it not been for my determination to prove to him *and to myself* that I *could* and *would* survive without him, my heart would probably still be a tattered mess waiting for him to resuscitate it. As the song says, "But for the amazing grace of God, there go I." Although I'm not proud of the stuff I did to hold on to this man, I am proud of how I was able to pull myself back up, dust myself off, and move on *without* him.

I almost lost me trying to keep this man, but some of you may be on the verge of losing yourselves trying to find or hold on to something or somebody, too. It may not be a boyfriend or a "significant other." It may be a mother or a father, but you have to know that love does not hurt; it heals. This man showed me that if it causes more pain than it does comfort, you're probably better off without it.

I'm not bitter about the end of my relationship with

this man, and I harbor no ill feelings towards him because I was a very willing participant *and* he taught me lessons that I'll never forget. It's because of him that I know love shouldn't hurt. He taught me that when love does hurt, it's best to let it go – even if letting go hurts more. It was he taught me that mental strength is much more valuable than physical strength. Because of him, I know just how strong I really am. Once you understand your own worth, you'll see the merit in my words. You'll believe that you can demand more because you'll know you deserve more; and if/when anybody refuses to give you your "more," you can walk away and *still* live in your truth because by then you will have also accepted that the *only* Being you *really* need in your life is God Almighty. You will be able to walk in your truth because He will never leave nor forsake you, no matter what you've done; and He will never cause you to question your worth. If anything, He will show you just how worthy you really are.

I hope my words find their mark and help you in

some way on your road to self-discovery and self-love.

Thanks again for your attention and your patronage.

With love, Miss Moe

.

YOU Can't Tell MY Story

Stacy L. Moore

YOU can't tell MY story

'cause it ain't your story to tell.

You can't wear my scars 'cause they're badges of honor

and you may not wear them quite as well.

Your story's all yours,

but this one is all mine -

the plot, the characters, even the ever-changing endings

that sometimes cross that imaginary line.

YOU can't tell MY story

'cause it ain't your story to tell.

You can't barter my emotions

as if they're part of some hot tabloid for sale.

My story's complex.

It's nowhere close to being an open book.

You won't be able to understand my plight

with one quick look.

YOU can't tell MY story

'cause it ain't your story to tell.

You can't recreate my setting

to try and make it a nice place to dwell.

You can't recognize my story

through the smiles or tears on my face.

You can't simply look at me

and assume you know how I ended up in this place.

YOU can't tell MY story

'cause it ain't your story to tell.

You can't undo what's been done

and pretend that everything in my world is well.

You can't carry my bag

for it may be a tad bit too heavy.

You can't auction my burdensome load

and impose your own unique kind of levy.

YOU can't tell MY story

'cause it ain't your story to tell.

I've worn my battle scars with pride,

so now I have the right to stand strong and tall.

Reflections

As a teacher, I am trained to ensure a student's comprehension before I move to a new lesson. Therefore, on the following pages, you are asked to think about the subjects that we covered in the previous six lessons **and** discuss what you took away from each one of them. I won't be able to read your work, but you should still think about the pieces of information that stood out to you and *why*.

I hope this process will make things clearer to you. Again, thank you for your consideration and your patronage. I am eternally grateful for your kindness.

Stacy

Lesson 1: Know you're worthy!

List **two** things to which you could relate in this lesson and explain why you chose those two things.

1.

_____

_____

_____

_____

_____

_____

_____

_____

_____

_____

_____

_____

_____

_____

2.

_____

_____

_____

_____

_____

_____

_____

_____

_____

_____

_____

_____

_____

_____

_____

_____

_____

Lesson 2: Eliminate excuses!

List **two** things to which you could relate in this lesson and explain why you chose those two things.

1.

_____

_____

_____

_____

_____

_____

_____

_____

_____

_____

_____

_____

_____

_____

_____

_____

_____

_____

_____

_____

_____

_____

_____

_____

_____

_____

_____

_____

_____

_____

_____

2. _____

_____

_____

_____

_____

_____

_____

_____

_____

_____

_____

_____

_____

_____

_____

_____

_____

_____

_____

_____

Lesson 3: Keep your circle small!

List **two** things to which you could relate in this lesson and explain why you chose those two things.

1.

2.

_____

_____

_____

_____

_____

_____

_____

_____

_____

_____

_____

_____

_____

_____

_____

_____

_____

_____

_____

_____

_____

_____

_____

_____

_____

_____

_____

_____

_____

_____

_____

_____

_____

_____

_____

Lesson 4: Everybody makes mistakes; don't let yours define you!

List **two** things to which you could relate in this lesson and explain why you chose those two things.

1.

_____

_____

_____

_____

_____

_____

_____

_____

_____

_____

_____

_____

2.

_____

_____

_____

_____

_____

_____

_____

_____

_____

_____

_____

_____

_____

_____

_____

_____

_____

_____

Lesson 5: Don't let others use you!

List **two** things to which you could relate in this lesson and explain why you chose those two things.

1.

_____

_____

_____

_____

_____

_____

_____

_____

_____

_____

_____

_____

_____

_____

_____

_____

_____

_____

_____

_____

_____

_____

_____

_____

_____

_____

_____

_____

_____

_____

_____

_____

2.

LESSONS LIFE TAUGHT ME

_____

_____

_____

_____

_____

_____

_____

_____

_____

_____

_____

_____

_____

_____

_____

_____

_____

_____

Lesson 6: Don't lose you trying to keep him!

List **two** things to which you could relate in this lesson and explain why you chose those two things.

1.

_____

_____

_____

_____

_____

_____

_____

_____

_____

_____

_____

_____

_____

_____

_____

_____

_____

_____

_____

_____

_____

_____

_____

_____

_____

_____

_____

_____

_____

_____

_____

_____

2.

ABOUT THE AUTHOR

Stacy L. Moore, affectionately known to her students as "Miss Moe," is a lifelong resident of Pattison, MS, a small rural town where everybody literally knows everybody. Stacy has spent the last 20 years teaching in the same school district she attended as a child and says she would not rather teach anywhere else in the world. A graduate of Port Gibson High School, Stacy received her bachelor's and master's degrees in English from Tougaloo College and Alcorn State University respectively. She was named *Star Teacher* in both 2013 and 2015 for her dedication to education and her non-conventional techniques for reaching students. Stacy is the mother of one son, Jhmarquias Newsome, and "Granny" to three: grandson Kody and granddaughters A'Zylia and Peyton. This is Stacy's first book, and although she says, "It was like being in *labor* all over again," she's not opposed to the idea of writing at least one more.

Made in the USA
Columbia, SC
13 May 2020